Race
You are the winner as per your state.

S Afrose

Ukiyoto Publishing

All global publishing rights are held by

Ukiyoto Publishing

Published in 2024

Content Copyright © S Afrose

ISBN 9789362690623

All rights reserved.

No part of this publication may be reproduced, transmitted, or stored in a retrieval system, in any form by any means, electronic, mechanical, photocopying, recording or otherwise, without the prior permission of the publisher.

The moral rights of the author have been asserted.

This is a work of fiction. Names, characters, businesses, places, events, locales, and incidents are either the products of the author's imagination or used in a fictitious manner. Any resemblance to actual persons, living or dead, or actual events is purely coincidental.

This book is sold subject to the condition that it shall not by way of trade or otherwise, be lent, resold, hired out or otherwise circulated, without the publisher's prior consent, in any form of binding or cover other than that in which it is published.

www.ukiyoto.com

Dedication

To all the people,
Who fight each moment
For taking the breath.

Without any fear,
Full of stresses,
Can't hold their steps.

Believe for living,
This art-
You are the winner,
As per your own state, dear.

Acknowledgement

Thanks a lot Dear Almighty for blessing me always.
Thank you so much dear parents, friends, readers, well-wishers.
You, all are my supporters, my dear world.

My paradise of words, is my dear heart, full of compassions and love.
There's only one life. We have to make sure about its core of heart. Don't be in the painful phase. Don't destroy the dreamy hub. This is the race on the earth. Don't be shocked for being a loser. You are the winner, my dear.

Love for all, from the deepest core of my heart.

From Author Desk
© **S Afrose**
Dhaka, Bangladesh, (18th May'24).

Hello! Can you hear me?

Race!
The flag is flying
Ready!
Go.

It's your turn
You have been playing
For a long period.

Now it's time
To make sure
The medal as the icon of winner,
Must be welcome by yourself.

Don't worry dear.
A bit fear.
Damn it!
You will be doomed anyway,
If think so much.

Just focus on the goal.
You will hold
The gem
Of your own life.

That's great
You are the winner.
Believe this
You have made this time,
Doing your best.
Just accept and beat each challenge.

Life itself is the Race.
You are the racer.

We are racers.
We can't deny.
We can't forget this part.

**" Race... Be your smile with the winning sigh.
That's the original racer."**

Preface

Race! Ready for the stage. Don't go back. You know that- The world is the big platform. Life is the race. You are the racer. There are so many steps. Gradually you will go. Ups-downs! Loser or Winner! OOPS!

What's the matter? First, come to the point. You are the winner as per your state, don't forget this.

Race... a poetry book, containing so many words, as the beads of the garland.

So nice. Let's enjoy. Care and share with your dearself.

As for example- Race, Through the dark, Flying motion, Direction etc.

Hope you will enjoy this book. Take this one as a part of your favourite heart. Love & love.

(For any kind of unwanted words, just pardon.)

Thanks!

From Author Desk ♥

©S Afrose, Bangladesh. **(18th May'24)**

Let's Start the RACE:

Contents

Race	1
Mystery	2
Midnight dance	3
Get you	4
That art	5
Through the dark	7
Flying motion	8
Hip-hop hurray	9
Dancing with the time	11
Direction	12
Icy touch	13
Take this gift	14
New fragrance	15
Not familiar	16
That essence	17
Blocked dreams	19
Nightmares	20
A tiny hope	21
Fire and fire	23
Rainbow Umbrella	24
Who does care?	25
The new passage	27
A passion	28
Basket Ball	29
Who can feel?	30
Find out for me	31
Audition	32

Auditorium	33
Open the bottle	36
Time to relax mind	38
Identify	40
The fierce sound	41
Place the mind	43
Hahahahaha	44
Really?	45
Can't wait	46
Looking so far	47
You know that	48
I lose my way	49
Nobody knows	50
The sweet fragrance	51
You just stop	52
They are here	53
Joy of life	54
Red and Green	55
The cute baby	56
Wolf Girl	57
The Fantasy ride	59
Several attempts	60
The big canvas of life	62
Crying bird	63
Sewing each pore	64
Hidden Spirit	65
About the Author	70

Race

But, what's this step?
Race?
What's that?

Competition,
Always
On-going.

At each step.
Strange?
Never.

Life is the biggest Race
We are racers.
We play always.

Our designed arts.
Make those,
Our own choices.

(24th Mar-24)

Mystery

Top to bottom
A story,
Very soon
Well known-
A history.

Mystery!
Mystery!

Topic for what?
A letter, A life,
A new look,
A new uniform.

A new universe.
Unexpected?
Not right.

Have been writing,
For being cheating,
Cheapest words.
Mystery!
Always is here.

(28th Mar-24)

Midnight dance

Let's enjoy this moment.
Sober view?
Never.

Midnight dance.
All the time,
Called the sense.

A cup of milk,
A cup of coffee,
And then?

Let's try.
Let's make this time,
Who is in the real sense?

Midnight dance,
With all stars
And the beautiful moon's smile.

(28th Mar-24)

Get you

Thanks for your vision.
Tattoo of my heart.

Thanks for your words.
Not clear all over.

Got it.
Pick the point.

Get you,
Application of the mind.

Never lose,
When tears come without any concern.

(28th Mar-24)

That art

Now it's the right time
Greetings dear.

Now it's not the right time.
Greetings dear.

How funny!
Showing lame causes.

That art-
It's here for a long time.

Waiting
For something.

Waiting
For someone.

Who can guess?
That art.

It is here
For its happiness.

It's here

For its owner.

For the real colour,
For the real painter.

(28th Mar-24)

Through the dark

Let's show up
Ardent muse of earth,
Ardent words.

Through the dark!

Let's meet
Together,
Holding hands of love.
Ardent desires.

Through the dark
Let's make this ride,
Ardent mind
Can't give up.

Make this earth.
What do you want?
Ardent pleasure.
Ardent weather.

(28th Mar-24)

Flying motion

Capture this caption
Flying motion.

Flying hair
Flying everywhere.

Making her
A little pie.

Straight forward
Never late, dear.

Capture this vision
Your caption.

You are here
The vehicle of the life.

(28th Mar-24)

Hip-hop hurray

Don't make this pace
A new race.

Obviously
It's the race.

The race of life.
Wow!

Just enough.
Just enjoy.

Hip-hop hurray!
Hip-hop hurray!

I enjoy.
I love.

Do you?
Will you?

Just care.
Just share.

Everything turns,

Even facing the daring part.

(28th Mar-24)

Dancing with the time

He is near the end of life
He has been writing the rhyme,
I will ensure this part
My friend, my favourite art.

Dancing with the time.
He makes his decision all over.
The only life has been ruining,
I will not take it over.

I will make this moment.
Ensure the fragrance.
The frame of life,
Dancing with the time.

(3rd Apr-24)

Direction

East or West
North or South,
Each different part
Each direction.

Make this vault.
You know,
Haunted.
Why?

Misleading.
Misinformation,
Making a false passion.

Stop
And then think,
The proper direction.

(3rd Apr-24)

Icy touch

A cooler
Zipped.

The beautiful journey
The rose lane.
The white rose.

Quick update.
No way,
The icy touch.

The rose
On the ice land,
No way.

The rose
Missing,
The warmth touch overall.

(3rd Apr-24)

Take this gift

A simple sign
Take my love
My warmth greetings!

A rose
With my heart.
Take this gift.

I wish
Your overall success,
Without being upset,
Just accept.

Hope you will understand
And then,
Say-
Will you take this time?

(3rd Apr-24)

New fragrance

Doomed the life,
At last.

No!
It can't wait anymore.

So?
A new fragrance.

Lavender lane.
Lavender hues.

Lavender mind.
Lavender love.

Making this sense
A new fragrance,
Need to cope
Don't act as the stupid one.

(3rd Apr-24)

Not familiar

After accessing this part
The race of the life,
Winner, Hurray!
Don't blame me for your loss, dear.
Not familiar.

Walking cautiously
For reaching the place,
After that
You can't blame.
How can make?

When I love
To say To walk,
Don't force me
To say you,
So what?

Even the earth
Can't stop
For a moment,
Who am I?
Will sit this afternoon, for getting the agile vibe?

(3rd Apr-24)

That essence

Once
A little prank
A little girl,
Midnight dance
That ball room.

Decided
To destroy
The beautiful mind,
That ball room.
How strange!

So far
Anything Anytime.
That little girl
With her piano,
Painting the song of mind.

By each note
By each button,
Her piano
Is the witness,
For her vault.

Her smile

Race

Her happiness
Is not here,
All the time
She is the simple guy.

Decorated room
Now lost.
No one sings.
No shining part,
Vault of mind.

She is where?
Nobody can say.
Share dear
Wipe tears,
Witness of fear.

Look at there
The piano, the picture,
Still the same.
You must believe
That essence.

(3rd Apr-24)

Blocked dreams

Dazzling views
Sparkling night.
Dark sky.
Ray of what?

Blocked dreams.
Blocked dreams.

Credit card!
No coins.
Oh no!
So sorry.

Can't free
Dearest dreams,
Blocked cage,
Blocked the dream.

Need some more
Making the pore,
To release arts,
No blockage dear.

(3rd Apr-24)

Nightmares

So?
Hissssss?
A heart breaking sound.
Nightmares!

Ouch!
A big punch
To my chest,
Broken the rest.

Nightmares!
Don't care.
Dare to come?
Hahahahahaha!

Chill!
Let it face
With daring face.
Nightmares!

(3rd Apr-24)

A tiny hope

That phase
On the sky,
A big hole
A tiny hope.
The tunnel.

Tunnel for life
Tunnel for mind,
Tunnel forever
Tunnel for dreams.

Basically
Not read,
No reply.
Rush for what?

The race
Face to face,
Dare to taste
Test of mind.

Race

Task not finished,
Making it's possible,
When can see
A tiny hope.

(3rd Apr-24)

Fire and fire

Make sure this time,
Fire and fire.

Even is not everywhere,
Forward to Backward.

Fire and fire,
I thought this.

Bow to Him.
Easily chase.

You, the chaser,
Making it clear.

Fire and fire
Day to night,,, the Tire.

(3rd Apr-24)

Rainbow Umbrella

Rain
Rainbow!
Rainy dance.

Rainbow Umbrella!
Tiny to big
Some of them,
Visible.

Visit the time
Drops of mind,
Rain can't check
Its prospect.

They are here
As the safe guards,
Just need to show
And wear the shirt.

With drops of rain
With drops of love,
Wow!
Rainbow Umbrella.

(3rd Apr-24)

Who does care?

Anything here?
Who can care?
Who can share?
Whole the life
Theory of heart-

Who does care?

Should I?
Many mistakes.
Many times,
A game... oops!
Lost project of life.

Who will share?
Who is near?
Who can peep?
Who is there?
The Melody!

Who does care?

The cart is empty
The way is here,
Despite any rush

Pushing the heart.
Pls don't say this anymore-

Who does care?

(2nd Apr'24)

The new passage

Not so easy
When you see,
The gate.

He knew that
The new passage,
Instead of the fact.

So?
Let the world know
It's the time.

Make the way.
Full of mystery?
Never mind.

The new passage
For the fact,
All of you, dear.

(27th Apr-24)

A passion

Make it
And go,

The race is ahead.

Know it
And absorb,

The reason is unknown.

Cage!
Just chase.

Race! It's the race,
And then share the real pace.

(27th Apr-24)

Basket Ball

The ball
On the playground.
So many players.
Among them
You are scared,
And then?

Sweating!
You can't be here.
Anyway.
You have designed
Your own state.
Now what?

Basket Ball!
You want to play.
Want to be the winner.
Then make it possible
And of course,
Will be with your smile.

(17th Apr-24)

Who can feel?

The basket is empty
The basket is not empty.

Two answers.
Who can guess?

The next step
The upcoming project.

Who can feel?
Actually it's the abstract reel.

(17th Apr-24)

Find out for me

It's okay.
You can go
And find out,
Those answers
For me.

Only for me,
Find out for me.

The diversity.
Oh no!
I don't think so.
Let's try
For the other part.

Find out the way for me
Find out the truth for me.

(17th Apr-24)

Audition

Audition,
That's not my fault.
Vision,
That's not my ambition.

Audition
Full of cryptic arts.
Silly thoughts,
Can't give up.

Audition!
Be careful at a time,
Otherwise,
The collapsed art.

(17th Apr-24)

Auditorium

May I come in?
Yes!

What do you want?
To participate.

Player?
No, the public side, as a visitor.

I see.
Ticket?

No one.
Why?

No money.
Then?

Can see you later.
Possible or not?

What do you mean?
I want to be there-
The Auditorium.

That is asking by me.
I can hear.
I have to sit there.
Pls help me this time.

No way.
Hmmm!

Side to side
Whisper of minds.

Excuse me!
I am the player of the race 2022 Dec-23.

May I ask for the gate pass?
Oh!

Pls
Here's the pass.

Go ahead
And enjoy the show.

The game is running,
Mind is seeking.

How funny!

Anything?

The Auditorium
Is full of so many people.

I go there
And simply sit on the seat.

Then say-
Do your best.

(17th Apr-24)

Open the bottle

Dream?
Sleeping.
Sky?
Peeping.

Sun
Asking,
Am I
Rising?

Wave
Dancing.
Cloud
Coughing.

Time
laughing.
Dream
Seeking.

See there
A bottle,
Inside?

Something hanging.

Dream!
Dream!
Open the bottle
Hug me dear babydoll.

(18th May-24)

Time to relax mind

Lost the state,
Broken road,
Silly door,
And?

Now a billboard,
A sentence is hanging
Can't you see?
How do you feel?

Time to relax mind,
For the maintenance
Rhythms of life,
Race of casting role?

Stuck?
Not accepted.
Close eyes for a new earth,
The door is alright.

Ready for your turn
No excuse my dear
You have to do this moment

As you are on the race.

Take some moments
It's fine,
Time to relax mind
Sober!

(18th May-24)

Identify

Pls!
Just anytime,
Time?
Identify.

Real name.
Real Identity.
Many more.
Oops!

Value
And then,
Roll
The life.

(5th May-24)

The fierce sound

From so far
It comes,
Shoes on legs.
What?

The fierce sound.
My dear crown!
My dear pie!
How nice!

Make me
Feel me,
Am I right?
Fierce for what?

You know that
I can set,
What's the matter?
Ready for that part.

Meanwhile managed,
Then the sound,
Ouch!
Collapsed.

(5th May-24)

Place the mind

Forward
The lane.
The desired bridge,
The beautiful ride.

Place the mind
Get the point
And then,
You can realise.

Make it
Below the gist
You burned,
Now turn.

I see
You make this
So nice,
My dear pie.

(5th May-24)

Hahahahaha

Mind says
I am fine,
I enjoy
You can't imagine.
How fine!

Fume of heart.
My head,
My mind,
Oh dear!

Hahahahah!
The sound
Coming,
And then access the site.

Figure it out.
Love it
Believe it.
Hahahahah!

(5th May-24)

Really?

And then?
You cried
Why?

Lost the game.
The racer
Is on the life's back.

Really ?
Now what?
Love me.
Who is there?

No sense,
No essence,
No life.
Really?

(5th May-24)

Can't wait

When will that day come?
When will that happen?

Can't wait.

Sitting
As an observer.

Hope,
Everything is fine.

Really that, mind loves.
Thanks!

(5th May-24)

Looking so far

What do you see?
Don't know.

What do you get?
Don't know.

My part-
My art-

Wow!
Looking so far.

So?
That's my part.

My dear!
Don't know, why?

Now can say,
This is not my part.

(5th May-24)

You know that

But the fact
You know that,
The tattoo,
On your arms.
How can hide?

You know that,
You can't get.
Hit the rate,
You make that,
Now fit the stage.

(5th May-24)

I lose my way

Eyes
Can't be able to see.
Forward so dark.
Then,
How can proceed?

Lost the way.
I lose my way.

Eyes
Trying,
And then
Get the fact.
How can proceed?

I lose my way.
I am concerned about the fact.

(5th May-24)

Nobody knows

Even it's
So much famous,
You can't escape.
You can't deny.
Nobody knows.

Even
Greetings the heart,
There's the lack of rhythms.
Lack of blood.
Nobody knows.

I want,
I was.
Don't dare?
Saying?
Stop!

I will not
As I know,
Nobody knows.
Once was-
Now the same part.

(5th May-24)

The sweet fragrance

Making this sense
A new lane,
Mark this time
The sweet fragrance of the life.

Oh sweet heart!
Give it a part,
I know that,
This is not Sober.

(7th May-24)

You just stop

I love this time.
When you see
Then can get,
How nice!
Thanks a lot dear one.

Make this time.
I know I see,
I love the part.
How nice!

Dear one,
Dear heart,
Hi fi!
Don't feel shyness as usual.

(7th May-24)

They are here

Rare!
Never.

We are here.
So?

They are here,
They make peers.

They shed tears.
No dear.

They are here,
They are not Rare.

(7th May-24)

Joy of life

Unique this time.
Fine or shine?
Joy of mind.
Joy of life.

Unique essence.
This time,
This rhyme,
Joy of life.

Mark,
A new cascade.
You have seen,
Need to prepare.

Pray and say
Lay and lay,
The graveyard?
Oh no dear!

(7th May-24)

Red and Green

The alarm!
Don't make noise.

And take a break.

Meeting is fixed.
Now tell me,
What's in your mind?
Need to clear.

Clarify my thoughts.
My love my words,
Though I am here,
I love to hear.

(7th May-24)

The cute baby

He is a cute one,
Sitting on the chair.
Making a new trend
The cute baby.

He holds a device.
That is hidden from his sight,
Sign now-
Then make the cosmic bow.

(7th May-24)

Wolf Girl

Long ago
A decent rhyme,
Deepest the forest
A new pine.

A little one
Nobody is there,
As her beloved parts.
Ah!

She lives all alone
Work with her own tears,
Fighting each time,
As the lady chime.

A little doggy
Is her friend,
Without any fear
She will go to further.

What's that meaning?
A link or a jinx?
Need to clear.
Wolf girl!

Wow!
Not bad.
I like that.
Wolf girl.

Let's start
This is the new art.
How can progress?
A little girl?

(7th May-24)

The Fantasy ride

Once upon a time a beautiful girl
Made her dreams in the Fantasy world.
She was very much happy dear
Suddenly the appearance of the Demoniar.

She was lost her dream on earth
Her soul was stuck in that hub,
That made the new way of life
Then the beginning of the Fantasy ride.

Bow to the Dearest Lord
Giving me such amazing power,
For enjoying the life even after death
May be as a soul, so what? Angel!

Nothing can destroy that Fantasy world
She has been making her own path,
Who dares to come and snatch my Paradise?
He or she will be doomed anytime,Hahahaha!

(7th May-24)

Several attempts

Hot water
Hot sun
Hot head,
And?

Several attempts.
Several moments.

Meanwhile
It's managed,
Actually
Not the set.

Several attempts
You made,
Still
The downstairs race.

Forward?
How can?
Thinking-
Several attempts.

You know
Very well,
This is the Race

Trace.

Several attempts
Let it happen,
Become your trend,
Until the Gunpoint.

(18th May-24)

The big canvas of life

Surroundings so mesmerising
Message of heart,
The swing with the giant tree
The big canvas of life.

It hopes to fly
With its wings of mind,
Golden shade of life
Golden ray of earth.

Many leaves many dreams
Gradually fall gradually swing,
One by one with the time
Still surroundings can't be so familiar.

The swing calls
As the mind's vault,
With its root of smile
The tree is the big canvas of life.

(7th May-24)

Crying bird

Chirping sounds of heart
Crying bird,
So painful
This beautiful art.

The bird can't sing a song
Making a new port of life,
Hopefully this time
It will sing the song of love.

Crying bird.
Don't hide,
Lead the wonderful life
Crying is not the prime part.

(18th May-24)

Sewing each pore

Let it happen this time
Sewing each pore of cloth,
That is your favourite one
Don't go away my dear heart.

Each pore is not dear
Still is here to care,
Sewing and sewing
Love each part of that, my dear.

Know this time
Life is the race,
Game of dreams
Make a siren.

Ready
And respect,
Your each step
Still continue that sewing.

(18th May-24)

Another Essence:
Hidden Spirit

Time to get up. Hello! Hello! Are you hearing me? Hello!
It's continuing from the very past.
Who did make that call?
Who was there?
Who ???

A shadow! A real gem!
A caption- come on and enjoy this lane.

What's that meaning?
Don't understand.
Pls make it clear.
Fine.
Go there. The beautiful nature. The beautiful creatures are everywhere.
A little bit more. Just wait.
A little butterfly. Wow!
Hello dear fly!
Make me your friend.
I want to play with you.

The butterfly! It was not as like as, on the time of its birth.
It was a caterpillar. You didn't like. You didn't pay your attention. It cried a lot. A painful phase of life.
Then, gradually it comes out with its hidden spirits, for being the beautiful art on this earth. That is the most important thing. Time should be worthful, for this plot.
Now look,
Everyone loves it.

Everyone likes it.
It enjoys the life finally.

Change will come step by step, with its power to see the new venture of life.
Look at this little seed. It's hidden. Nobody can see. After careful touches, it comes out gradually with its supreme look,,, a big tree . Just wow! It has so many green leaves. It can be used as a shelter. It helps others by giving some of its sweet fruits and fragrance of breeze etc. So cool!

Is that possible from the very beginning?
No.

When it was a little plant, it cried.
" I can't help anyone. I have no strength to fight with the storm."
It cried a lot."
Then someone makes a call. The hidden spirit, the hidden power. That's the power to change, both physically and mentally.
When it believes that one, then life turns into a very different angle. It's the mandatory part of the dearest life. Nobody can deny this fact. Nobody can escape.
A newborn! It comes with the beautiful sound of its crying part. But people love.
When it can see and feel anything, the world is so amazing. Gradually it comes out, step by step, with the changing platform of the life.
A newborn, to a toddler. A toddler to a teenager, and then it's the on-going process of the life. Continues...

With time everything is going to change, mind can't focus on anymore. What's going on? Finally there's a time, when mind has

caged its spirit of the smile, the beauty of life.
Then the collapsed part shows up. Makes a horrible plot. Oh no! Metamorphosis is happening all the time. Nobody can stop it. It's the natural vibe. But the fact is, make its way for the desired lane. Let it help to feel and rise up with the hidden spirit, for changing the whole scenario of the dearest life. Obviously for the desired outcome.

Every life has its own prospect.

It has the hidden spirit. That will help to change the form or phase of the life's platform. It may take some more times.

But it must be happened. Just need to believe.

And ready for accepting the change of the life.

That will help to see the vast universe with a different shade and a different angle.

Muse of life can hear with the dreamy ride.

Just coordinate itself with the glamour of mind and truthful canvas of life.

Then everything will be the adorable moment, to move on without any hesitation.

(1st April'24)

"THANK YOU SO MUCH
FOR YOUR LOVE,
TOWARDS MY BEAUTIFUL CANVAS
<u>RACE</u>
RIGHT NOW.
BE YOUR DEARSELF"

© S AFROSE, BD.
(18th May-'24)

About the Author

S Afrose

Author S Afrose (Sabiha Afrose, from Bangladesh). She has been writing since Aug-2020. That was the first time to enter into the literature world.

From the various aspects of life, she has tried to make the way of inspiration, with the hopeful mind. Her each word reflects the thought of mind; using metaphoric vibes of the positivity. By this magical weapon of quill, she has been making her own world, reflection of the dearest mind.

Gradually it's turned into her passion, panacea, best friend.

Her writes have been publishing on Intl. magazines and anthologies (90+)

She has achieved so many awards and recognitions from various platforms of the literature (Poetry) world.

For example- Doctorate in Literature from Instituto Cultural Colombiano, Literoma Laureate Winner 2022, Mahatma Gandhi Award from Instituto Cultural Colombiano 2023, a proud member of the Hyperpoem Project of World Record Holder etc.

Those help her, making a strong basement. And that is, now her paradise.

There are 29 Poetry books available on Amazon Worldwide and also other sites, book stores etc.

Some of them are available here on Rokomari. Com, in BANGLADESH.

As for the native zone, there are some Bangla and English poetry books (published from Bangladesh)

Name of her published books are: Thanks Dear God, Poetic Essence, Reflection of Mind, Glittering Hopes, Angels Smile, Tiny Garden of Words, Dancing Alphabet, Artistic Muse, Essence of Love, Dear Children, Haunted Site, Woman, A Little Fantasy, The Butterfly, Lion's Roar, The Magical Quill, No War, Friendship, Lost Lotus, The Bride, A New Beginning, Bluish Ocean, Stop Discrimination, a Bouquet of Love, Golden Wings of Time, Dear Mother etc.

Her mother is Selina Begum and father is Manirul Islam. B Pharm, M Pharm from Jahangirnagar University, BD. Favourite hobbies are reading, writing, specially the poetry section. Born on 10th Dec-84, Narsingdi.

Contact-
afrosewritings@outlook.com
sabiha_pharma@yahoo.com
You Tube: S Afrose *Muse of Writes*(@safrose_poetic_arts)
Facebook page: Muse of Words by S Afrose
Twitter:@afrose2020
Inst. @safrosepoetryworld

www.ingramcontent.com/pod-product-compliance
Lightning Source LLC
LaVergne TN
LVHW041628070526
838199LV00052B/3276